INTRO

LIFE IS NOT ALWAYS RED ROSES, DARK CHOCOLATE SQUARES, AND LADY BUGS. SOMETIMES LIFE CONSISTS OF NO FLOWERS, NO CHOCOLATE CANDIES, AND MILLIONS OF FIRE-BREATHING PISS ANTS.

MOST GRATITUDE JOURNALS FOCUS ON THE POSITIVE WHILE LARGELY NEGLECTING ANYTHING NEGATIVE. THIS IS FINE AND ALL, BUT YOU CAN'T JUST IGNORE THE DARKNESS AND LEAVE IT TRAPPED INSIDE. IT WILL EAT YOU UP.

INTRODUCING RAGE PAGE, A JOURNAL THAT ALLOWS YOU TO VENT. USE THIS JOURNAL TO WRITE DOWN YOUR FRUSTRATIONS, ANGER, AND EVEN SADNESS. ONCE YOU ARE FINISHED, CONTINUE WRITING ON THE OPPOSITE PAGE, WITH A MORE POSITIVE OUTLOOK.

FACE THE DARKNESS THEN LIGHT THE PATH TO HAPPINESS.

DATE MONTH / DAY / YEAR
___/___/___

DAY OF THE WEEK:
_____

ASSHOLE OF THE DAY

////////////////////////////
_____
PERSON, PLACE, OR THING

COLOR IN YOUR RAGE LEVEL!

CLUSTERFUCK of the day!

_____
_____
_____
_____
_____
_____
_____

THESE THINGS MAKE ME WANT TO PUNCH MY PILLOW...

1) _____
2) _____
3) _____
4) _____

!

WORD OF THE DAY!

MORE *Shit*

CONTINUE VENTING AND/OR EXPLORE THE POSSIBILITY THAT THERE MIGHT ACTUALLY BE A SILVER-LINING IN ALL OF THIS.

_____

_____

_____

_____

_____

_____

What Can I do to unclusterfuck tomorrow?

_____

_____

_____

_____

_____

_____

_____

_____

_____

_____

_____

I'M FUCKING LUCKY TO HAVE...

LIST PEOPLE AND/OR THINGS THAT YOU ARE GRATEFUL FOR.

1.
2.
3.
4.
5.

HAPPY THOUGHT OF THE DAY...

"IT CAN'T GET ANY WORSE.
BUT WE'LL DO OUR BEST."

DATE
_____ / _____ / _____

DAY OF THE WEEK:

ASSHOLE OF THE DAY

//

PERSON, PLACE, OR THING

COLOR IN YOUR RAGE LEVEL!

CLUSTERFUCK of the day!

_____
_____
_____
_____
_____
_____

THESE THINGS MAKE ME WANT TO PUNCH MY PILLOW...

1) _____
2) _____
3) _____
4) _____

!

WORD OF THE DAY!

MORE *Shit*

CONTINUE VENTING AND/OR EXPLORE THE POSSIBILITY THAT THERE MIGHT ACTUALLY BE A SILVER-LINING IN ALL OF THIS.

_____
_____
_____
_____
_____
_____
_____
_____

What Can I do to unclusterfuck tomorrow?

_____
_____
_____
_____
_____
_____
_____
_____
_____
_____
_____
_____

I'M FUCKING LUCKY TO HAVE...

LIST PEOPLE AND/OR THINGS THAT YOU ARE GRATEFUL FOR.

1.
2.
3.
4.
5.

HAPPY THOUGHT OF THE DAY...

DATE

_____ / _____ / _____

DAY OF THE WEEK: _____

Cumtart of the Day

//

PERSON, PLACE, OR THING

RAGE METER

COLOR IN YOUR RAGE LEVEL!

SHITFEST of the day!

_____

_____

_____

_____

_____

_____

_____

♫ CRAPPY DAY MUSIC PLAYLIST...

!

1) _____

2) _____

3) _____

4) _____

WORD OF THE DAY!

MORE *Shit*

CONTINUE VENTING AND/OR EXPLORE THE POSSIBILITY THAT THERE MIGHT ACTUALLY BE A SILVER-LINING IN ALL OF THIS.

What Can I do to unclusterfuck tomorrow?

GET SHIT DONE!
ACCOMPLISHING TASKS ARE A GREAT WAY TO FEEL BETTER. LIST THINGS THAT NEED TO GET DONE & DO IT!

1.
2.
3.
4.
5.

HAPPY THOUGHT OF THE DAY...

DATE ___ MONTH / ___ DAY / ___ YEAR

DAY OF THE WEEK:

DICKWEED OF THE DAY

PERSON, PLACE, OR THING

RAGE METER

FLAME MONSTER'S BITCH
FLAME MONSTER
FIREBREATHER
FIRECRACKER
SMALL FRY
POP-IT

COLOR IN YOUR RAGE LEVEL!

TRAINWRECK of the day!

THESE THINGS MAKE ME

1) _____
2) _____
3) _____
4) _____

WORD OF THE DAY!

MORE *Shit*

CONTINUE VENTING AND/OR EXPLORE THE POSSIBILITY THAT THERE MIGHT ACTUALLY BE A SILVER-LINING IN ALL OF THIS.

What Can I do to unclusterfuck tomorrow?

THESE WORDS MAKE ME HAPPY...

1.
2.
3.
4.
5.

HAPPY THOUGHT OF THE DAY...

DATE MONTH / DAY / YEAR
____ / ____ / ____

DAY OF THE WEEK: _____

FUCKFACE OF THE DAY

//////////////////////////////////

PERSON, PLACE, OR THING

RAGE METER

SWAT   PUNCH   NUKE

DRAW IN THE NEEDLE!

SHITSTORM of the day!

_____
_____
_____
_____
_____
_____
_____

I DON'T GIVE A RAT'S ASS ABOUT...

1) _____
2) _____
3) _____
4) _____

!

WORD OF THE DAY!

MORE *Shit*

CONTINUE VENTING AND/OR EXPLORE THE POSSIBILITY THAT THERE MIGHT ACTUALLY BE A SILVER-LINING IN ALL OF THIS.

What Can I do to unclusterfuck tomorrow?

GET SHIT DONE!

ACCOMPLISHING TASKS ARE A GREAT WAY TO FEEL BETTER. LIST THINGS THAT NEED TO GET DONE & DO IT!

1.
2.
3.
4.
5.

HAPPY THOUGHT OF THE DAY...

DAY OF THE WEEK:

Bitch of the Day

PERSON, PLACE, OR THING

RAGE METER

FIRE

HOT

MILD

COLOR IN YOUR RAGE LEVEL!

FLUSTERCLUCK of the day!

RELEASE FRUSTRATION. SCRIBBLE LIKE MAD!

!

WORD OF THE DAY!

MORE *Shit*

CONTINUE VENTING AND/OR EXPLORE THE POSSIBILITY THAT THERE MIGHT ACTUALLY BE A SILVER-LINING IN ALL OF THIS.

_____

_____

_____

_____

_____

What Can I do to unclusterfuck tomorrow?

_____

_____

_____

_____

_____

_____

_____

_____

_____

_____

_____

THESE _____ MAKE ME FEEL HAPPY.

1.
2.
3.
4.
5.

HAPPY THOUGHT OF THE DAY...

 **DATE** MONTH / DAY / YEAR ___ / ___ / ___

DAY OF THE WEEK:

ASSHOLE OF THE DAY

//////////////////////////////////////

PERSON, PLACE, OR THING

RAGE-O-METER

COLOR IN YOUR RAGE LEVEL!

 **CLUSTERFUCK** of the day!

_____
_____
_____
_____
_____
_____
_____

THESE THINGS MAKE ME WANT TO PUNCH MY PILLOW...

1) _____
2) _____
3) _____
4) _____

 **WORD OF THE DAY!**

MORE *Shit*

CONTINUE VENTING AND/OR EXPLORE THE POSSIBILITY THAT THERE MIGHT ACTUALLY BE A SILVER-LINING IN ALL OF THIS.

_____

_____

_____

_____

_____

_____

_____

_____

What Can I do to unclusterfuck tomorrow?

_____

_____

_____

_____

_____

_____

_____

_____

_____

_____

_____

_____

_____

I'M FUCKING LUCKY TO HAVE...

LIST PEOPLE AND/OR THINGS THAT YOU ARE GRATEFUL FOR.

1.
2.
3.
4.
5.

HAPPY THOUGHT OF THE DAY...

DATE MONTH / DAY / YEAR

____ / ____ / ____

DAY OF THE WEEK: _____

Cumtart of the Day

//////////////////////////////////////

PERSON, PLACE, OR THING

RAGE METER

COLOR IN YOUR RAGE LEVEL!

SHITFEST of the day!

_____
_____
_____
_____
_____
_____
_____

♫ CRAPPY DAY MUSIC PLAYLIST... ♫

1) _____
2) _____
3) _____
4) _____

!

WORD OF THE DAY!

MORE *Shit*

CONTINUE VENTING AND/OR EXPLORE THE POSSIBILITY THAT THERE MIGHT ACTUALLY BE A SILVER-LINING IN ALL OF THIS.

_____

_____

_____

_____

_____

_____

What Can I do to unclusterfuck tomorrow?

_____

_____

_____

_____

_____

_____

_____

_____

_____

_____

_____

GET SHIT DONE!
ACCOMPLISHING TASKS ARE A GREAT WAY TO FEEL BETTER. LIST THINGS THAT NEED TO GET DONE & DO IT!

1.

2.

3.

4.

5.

HAPPY THOUGHT OF THE DAY...

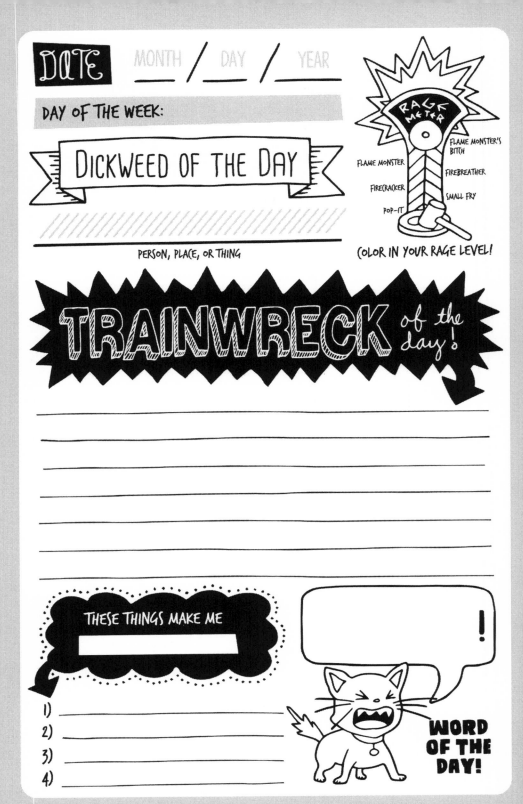

MORE *Shit*

CONTINUE VENTING AND/OR EXPLORE THE POSSIBILITY THAT THERE MIGHT ACTUALLY BE A SILVER-LINING IN ALL OF THIS.

What Can I do to unclusterfuck tomorrow?

THESE WORDS MAKE ME HAPPY...

1.
2.
3.
4.
5.

HAPPY THOUGHT OF THE DAY...

DATE

DAY OF THE WEEK:

FUCKFACE OF THE DAY

PERSON, PLACE, OR THING

500
400
300
200
100

RAGE METER

COLOR IN YOUR RAGE LEVEL!

SHITSTORM of the day!

I DON'T GIVE A RAT'S ASS ABOUT...

1)
2)
3)
4)

!

WORD OF THE DAY!

MORE *Shit*

CONTINUE VENTING AND/OR EXPLORE THE POSSIBILITY THAT THERE MIGHT ACTUALLY BE A SILVER-LINING IN ALL OF THIS.

_____
_____
_____
_____
_____
_____

What Can I do to unclusterfuck tomorrow?

_____
_____
_____
_____
_____
_____
_____
_____
_____
_____
_____
_____
_____
_____

GET SHIT DONE!

ACCOMPLISHING TASKS ARE A GREAT WAY TO FEEL BETTER. LIST THINGS THAT NEED TO GET DONE & DO IT!

1.
2.
3.
4.
5.

HAPPY THOUGHT OF THE DAY...

MORE *Shit*

CONTINUE VENTING AND/OR EXPLORE THE POSSIBILITY THAT THERE MIGHT ACTUALLY BE A SILVER-LINING IN ALL OF THIS.

_____

_____

_____

_____

_____

_____

What Can I do to unclusterfuck tomorrow?

THESE [   ] MAKE ME FEEL HAPPY.

1. _____
2. _____
3. _____
4. _____
5. _____

_____

_____

_____

_____

_____

_____

_____

_____

_____

_____

HAPPY THOUGHT OF THE DAY...

DATE ___ MONTH / ___ DAY / ___ YEAR

DAY OF THE WEEK:

ASSHOLE OF THE DAY

//

PERSON, PLACE, OR THING

COLOR IN YOUR RAGE LEVEL!

RAGE-O-METER

CLUSTERFUCK of the day!

_____
_____
_____
_____
_____
_____

THESE THINGS MAKE ME WANT TO PUNCH MY PILLOW...

1) _____
2) _____
3) _____
4) _____

!

WORD OF THE DAY!

MORE *Shit*

CONTINUE VENTING AND/OR EXPLORE THE POSSIBILITY THAT THERE MIGHT ACTUALLY BE A SILVER-LINING IN ALL OF THIS.

What Can I do to unclusterfuck tomorrow?

I'M FUCKING LUCKY TO HAVE...
LIST PEOPLE AND/OR THINGS THAT YOU ARE GRATEFUL FOR.

1.
2.
3.
4.
5.

HAPPY THOUGHT OF THE DAY...

DAY OF THE WEEK:

Cumtart of the Day

//

PERSON, PLACE, OR THING

COLOR IN YOUR RAGE LEVEL!

RA GE METER

SHITFEST of the day!

_____
_____
_____
_____
_____
_____
_____

CRAPPY DAY MUSIC PLAYLIST...

1) _____
2) _____
3) _____
4) _____

!

WORD OF THE DAY!

MORE *Shit*

CONTINUE VENTING AND/OR EXPLORE THE POSSIBILITY THAT THERE MIGHT ACTUALLY BE A SILVER-LINING IN ALL OF THIS.

_____

_____

_____

_____

_____

_____

_____

What Can I do to unclusterfuck tomorrow?

GET SHIT DONE!

ACCOMPLISHING TASKS ARE A GREAT WAY TO FEEL BETTER. LIST THINGS THAT NEED TO GET DONE & DO IT?

1.
2.
3.
4.
5.

HAPPY THOUGHT OF THE DAY...

DATE   MONTH / DAY / YEAR
___ / ___ / ___

DAY OF THE WEEK:
_____

DICKWEED OF THE DAY

////////////////////////////////////

PERSON, PLACE, OR THING

RAGE METER

FLAME MONSTER'S BITCH
FLAME MONSTER
FIREBREATHER
FIRECRACKER
SMALL FRY
POP-IT

COLOR IN YOUR RAGE LEVEL!

TRAINWRECK of the day!

_____
_____
_____
_____
_____
_____

THESE THINGS MAKE ME
_____

!

1) _____
2) _____
3) _____
4) _____

WORD OF THE DAY!

MORE *Shit*

CONTINUE VENTING AND/OR EXPLORE THE POSSIBILITY THAT THERE MIGHT ACTUALLY BE A SILVER-LINING IN ALL OF THIS.

_____

_____

_____

_____

_____

_____

What Can I do to unclusterfuck tomorrow?

_____

_____

_____

_____

_____

_____

_____

_____

_____

_____

_____

THESE WORDS MAKE ME HAPPY...

1.

2.

3.

4.

5.

HAPPY THOUGHT OF THE DAY...

DATE

DAY OF THE WEEK: _____

FUCKFACE OF THE DAY

//

PERSON, PLACE, OR THING

SWAT PUNCH NUKE

RAGE METER

DRAW IN THE NEEDLE!

SHITSTORM of the day!

_____
_____
_____
_____
_____
_____
_____

I DON'T GIVE A RAT'S ASS ABOUT...

1) _____
2) _____
3) _____
4) _____

!

WORD OF THE DAY!

MORE *Shit*

CONTINUE VENTING AND/OR EXPLORE THE POSSIBILITY THAT THERE MIGHT ACTUALLY BE A SILVER-LINING IN ALL OF THIS.

_____

_____

_____

_____

_____

_____

What Can I do to unclusterfuck tomorrow?

GET SHIT DONE!
ACCOMPLISHING TASKS ARE A GREAT WAY TO FEEL BETTER. LIST THINGS THAT NEED TO GET DONE & DO IT!

1.

2.

3.

4.

5.

_____

_____

_____

_____

_____

_____

_____

_____

_____

HAPPY THOUGHT OF THE DAY...

MONTH / DAY / YEAR
____ / ____ / ____

DAY OF THE WEEK:

Bitch of the Day

//

PERSON, PLACE, OR THING

RAGE METER

FIRE

HOT

MILD

COLOR IN YOUR RAGE LEVEL!

FLUSTERCLUCK of the day!

_____
_____
_____
_____
_____
_____

RELEASE FRUSTRATION.
SCRIBBLE LIKE MAD!

!

WORD OF THE DAY!

MORE *Shit*

CONTINUE VENTING AND/OR EXPLORE THE POSSIBILITY THAT THERE MIGHT ACTUALLY BE A SILVER-LINING IN ALL OF THIS.

_____
_____
_____
_____
_____
_____

What Can I do to unclusterfuck tomorrow?

_____
_____
_____
_____
_____
_____
_____
_____
_____
_____
_____

THESE [   ] MAKE ME FEEL HAPPY.

1.
2.
3.
4.
5.

HAPPY THOUGHT OF THE DAY...

DATE ___ MONTH / ___ DAY / ___ YEAR

DAY OF THE WEEK:

ASSHOLE OF THE DAY

PERSON, PLACE, OR THING

RAGE-O-METER

COLOR IN YOUR RAGE LEVEL!

CLUSTERFUCK of the day!

_____
_____
_____
_____
_____
_____
_____

THESE THINGS MAKE ME WANT TO PUNCH MY PILLOW...

1) _____
2) _____
3) _____
4) _____

!

WORD OF THE DAY!

MORE *Shit*

CONTINUE VENTING AND/OR EXPLORE THE POSSIBILITY THAT THERE MIGHT ACTUALLY BE A SILVER-LINING IN ALL OF THIS.

_____

_____

_____

_____

_____

_____

What Can I do to unclusterfuck tomorrow?

_____

_____

_____

_____

_____

_____

_____

_____

I'M FUCKING LUCKY TO HAVE...
LIST PEOPLE AND/OR THINGS THAT YOU ARE GRATEFUL FOR.

1.

2.

3.

4.

5.

HAPPY THOUGHT OF THE DAY...

DATE

MONTH / DAY / YEAR
____ / ____ / ____

DAY OF THE WEEK: _____

Cumtart of the Day

//////////////////////////////////////

PERSON, PLACE, OR THING

RAGE METER

COLOR IN YOUR RAGE LEVEL!

SHITFEST of the day!

_____
_____
_____
_____
_____
_____
_____

♫♪ CRAPPY DAY MUSIC PLAYLIST... ♫♪♪

!

1) _____
2) _____
3) _____
4) _____

WORD
OF THE
DAY!

MORE *Shit*

CONTINUE VENTING AND/OR EXPLORE THE POSSIBILITY THAT THERE MIGHT ACTUALLY BE A SILVER-LINING IN ALL OF THIS.

_____

_____

_____

_____

_____

_____

What Can I do to unclusterfuck tomorrow?

GET SHIT DONE!
ACCOMPLISHING TASKS ARE A GREAT WAY TO FEEL BETTER. LIST THINGS THAT NEED TO GET DONE & DO IT!

1. _____

2. _____

3. _____

4. _____

5. _____

_____

_____

_____

_____

_____

_____

_____

HAPPY THOUGHT OF THE DAY...

_____

_____

_____

DATE

___ / ___ / ___

DAY OF THE WEEK:

DICKWEED OF THE DAY

//

PERSON, PLACE, OR THING

RAGE METER

FLAME MONSTER'S BITCH

FLAME MONSTER

FIREBREATHER

FIRECRACKER

SMALL FRY

POP-IT

COLOR IN YOUR RAGE LEVEL!

TRAINWRECK of the day!

_____
_____
_____
_____
_____
_____
_____

THESE THINGS MAKE ME

_____

1) _____
2) _____
3) _____
4) _____

!

WORD OF THE DAY!

MORE Shit

CONTINUE VENTING AND/OR EXPLORE THE POSSIBILITY THAT THERE MIGHT ACTUALLY BE A SILVER-LINING IN ALL OF THIS.

_____
_____
_____
_____
_____
_____
_____

What Can I do to unclusterfuck tomorrow?

_____
_____
_____
_____
_____
_____
_____
_____
_____
_____

THESE WORDS MAKE ME HAPPY...

1.
2.
3.
4.
5.

HAPPY THOUGHT OF THE DAY...

DATE ___ MONTH / ___ DAY / ___ YEAR

DAY OF THE WEEK: _____

FUCKFACE OF THE DAY

/////////////////////////////////////

PERSON, PLACE, OR THING

500
400
300
200
100

RAGE METER

COLOR IN YOUR RAGE LEVEL!

SHITSTORM of the day!

_____
_____
_____
_____
_____
_____
_____

I DON'T GIVE A RAT'S ASS ABOUT...

1) _____
2) _____
3) _____
4) _____

!

WORD OF THE DAY!

MORE *Shit* CONTINUE VENTING AND/OR EXPLORE THE POSSIBILITY THAT THERE MIGHT ACTUALLY BE A SILVER-LINING IN ALL OF THIS.

_____
_____
_____
_____
_____
_____

What Can I do to unclusterfuck tomorrow?

GET SHIT DONE!
ACCOMPLISHING TASKS ARE A GREAT WAY TO FEEL BETTER. LIST THINGS THAT NEED TO GET DONE & DO IT!

1.
2.
3.
4.
5.

HAPPY THOUGHT OF THE DAY...

DATE

___ / ___ / ___

DAY OF THE WEEK:

Bitch of the Day

PERSON, PLACE, OR THING

NEED TO KILL SOMETHING!

BOILING OVER

ON EDGE

RAGE METER

COLOR IN YOUR RAGE LEVEL!

FLUSTERCLUCK of the day!

_____
_____
_____
_____
_____
_____

RELEASE FRUSTRATION. SCRIBBLE LIKE MAD!

!

WORD OF THE DAY!

MORE *Shit*

CONTINUE VENTING AND/OR EXPLORE THE POSSIBILITY THAT THERE MIGHT ACTUALLY BE A SILVER-LINING IN ALL OF THIS.

_____

_____

_____

_____

_____

_____

What Can I do to unclusterfuck tomorrow?

_____

_____

_____

_____

_____

_____

_____

_____

_____

_____

_____

_____

_____

THESE _____ MAKE ME FEEL HAPPY.

1.
2.
3.
4.
5.

HAPPY THOUGHT OF THE DAY...

DATE MONTH / DAY / YEAR
___ / ___ / ___

DAY OF THE WEEK:

ASSHOLE OF THE DAY

////////////////////
PERSON, PLACE, OR THING

RAGE-O-METER

COLOR IN YOUR RAGE LEVEL!

CLUSTERFUCK of the day!

_____
_____
_____
_____
_____
_____
_____

THESE THINGS MAKE ME WANT TO PUNCH MY PILLOW...

1) _____
2) _____
3) _____
4) _____

!

WORD OF THE DAY!

MORE Shit

CONTINUE VENTING AND/OR EXPLORE THE POSSIBILITY THAT THERE MIGHT ACTUALLY BE A SILVER-LINING IN ALL OF THIS.

_____
_____
_____
_____
_____
_____

What Can I do to unclusterfuck tomorrow?

_____
_____
_____
_____
_____
_____
_____
_____
_____
_____
_____

I'M FUCKING LUCKY TO HAVE...
LIST PEOPLE AND/OR THINGS THAT YOU ARE GRATEFUL FOR.

1.
2.
3.
4.
5.

HAPPY THOUGHT OF THE DAY...

MONTH / DAY / YEAR
____ / ____ / ____

DAY OF THE WEEK:

Cumtart of the Day

////////////////////////////////////

PERSON, PLACE, OR THING

RAGE METER

COLOR IN YOUR RAGE LEVEL!

SHITFEST of the day!

_____
_____
_____
_____
_____
_____
_____

♪ CRAPPY DAY MUSIC PLAYLIST... ♪♪

1) _____
2) _____
3) _____
4) _____

!

WORD OF THE DAY!

MORE *Shit*

CONTINUE VENTING AND/OR EXPLORE THE POSSIBILITY THAT THERE MIGHT ACTUALLY BE A SILVER-LINING IN ALL OF THIS.

_____

_____

_____

_____

_____

_____

What Can I do to unclusterfuck tomorrow?

_____

_____

_____

_____

_____

_____

_____

_____

_____

_____

_____

_____

_____

_____

GET SHIT DONE!
ACCOMPLISHING TASKS ARE A GREAT WAY TO FEEL BETTER. LIST THINGS THAT NEED TO GET DONE & DO IT!

1.

2.

3.

4.

5.

HAPPY THOUGHT OF THE DAY...

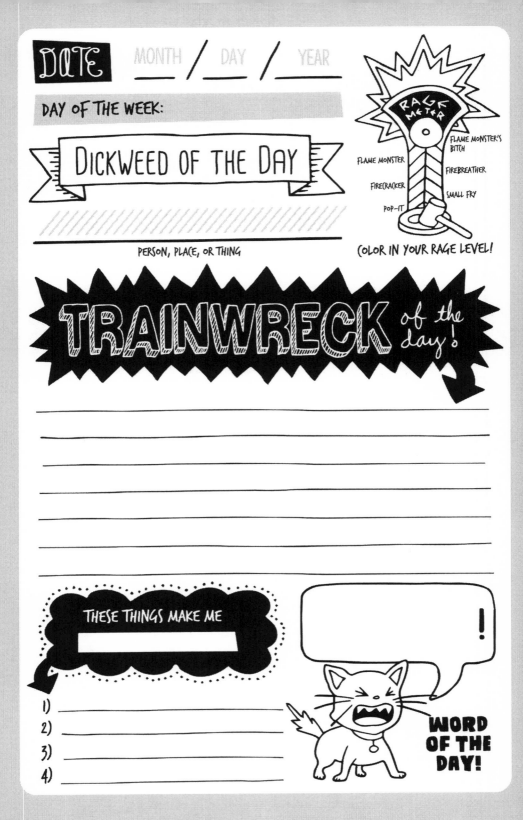

MORE Shit

CONTINUE VENTING AND/OR EXPLORE THE POSSIBILITY THAT THERE MIGHT ACTUALLY BE A SILVER-LINING IN ALL OF THIS.

_____

_____

_____

_____

_____

_____

What Can I do to unclusterfuck tomorrow?

_____

_____

_____

_____

_____

_____

_____

_____

_____

_____

_____

_____

_____

THESE WORDS MAKE ME HAPPY...

1.

2.

3.

4.

5.

HAPPY THOUGHT OF THE DAY...

DATE __ MONTH __ / __ DAY __ / __ YEAR __

DAY OF THE WEEK:

FUCKFACE OF THE DAY

PERSON, PLACE, OR THING

DRAW IN THE NEEDLE!

SHITSTORM of the day!

I DON'T GIVE A RAT'S ASS ABOUT...

1) _____
2) _____
3) _____
4) _____

WORD OF THE DAY!

MORE *Shit*

CONTINUE VENTING AND/OR EXPLORE THE POSSIBILITY THAT THERE MIGHT ACTUALLY BE A SILVER-LINING IN ALL OF THIS.

_____
_____
_____
_____
_____
_____

What Can I do to unclusterfuck tomorrow?

_____
_____
_____
_____
_____
_____
_____
_____
_____
_____
_____
_____
_____
_____
_____

GET SHIT DONE!

ACCOMPLISHING TASKS ARE A GREAT WAY TO FEEL BETTER. LIST THINGS THAT NEED TO GET DONE & DO IT!

1.
2.
3.
4.
5.

HAPPY THOUGHT OF THE DAY...

DATE ___ MONTH / ___ DAY / ___ YEAR

DAY OF THE WEEK: _____

Bitch of the Day

PERSON, PLACE, OR THING

RAGE METER
FIRE
HOT
MILD

COLOR IN YOUR RAGE LEVEL!

FLUSTERCLUCK of the day!

_____
_____
_____
_____
_____
_____
_____

RELEASE FRUSTRATION.
SCRIBBLE LIKE MAD!

!

WORD OF THE DAY!

MORE *Shit*

CONTINUE VENTING AND/OR EXPLORE THE POSSIBILITY THAT THERE MIGHT ACTUALLY BE A SILVER-LINING IN ALL OF THIS.

_____

_____

_____

_____

_____

_____

_____

What Can I do to unclusterfuck tomorrow?

_____

_____

_____

_____

_____

_____

_____

_____

_____

_____

_____

_____

THESE _____ MAKE ME FEEL HAPPY.

1.
2.
3.
4.
5.

HAPPY THOUGHT OF THE DAY...

DATE MONTH / DAY / YEAR
___ / ___ / ___

DAY OF THE WEEK: _____

ASSHOLE OF THE DAY

/////////////////////////////////

PERSON, PLACE, OR THING

RAGE-O-METER

COLOR IN YOUR RAGE LEVEL!

CLUSTERFUCK of the day!

_____
_____
_____
_____
_____
_____

THESE THINGS MAKE ME WANT TO
PUNCH MY PILLOW...

1) _____
2) _____
3) _____
4) _____

WORD OF THE DAY!

MORE *Shit*

CONTINUE VENTING AND/OR EXPLORE THE POSSIBILITY THAT THERE MIGHT ACTUALLY BE A SILVER-LINING IN ALL OF THIS.

What Can I do to unclusterfuck tomorrow?

I'M FUCKING LUCKY TO HAVE...
LIST PEOPLE AND/OR THINGS THAT YOU ARE GRATEFUL FOR.

1.
2.
3.
4.
5.

HAPPY THOUGHT OF THE DAY...

DATE MONTH / DAY / YEAR ___ / ___ / ___

DAY OF THE WEEK:

Cumtart of the Day

PERSON, PLACE, OR THING

COLOR IN YOUR RAGE LEVEL!

RAGE METER

SHITFEST of the day!

_____
_____
_____
_____
_____
_____

♫ CRAPPY DAY MUSIC PLAYLIST...

1) _____
2) _____
3) _____
4) _____

!

WORD OF THE DAY!

MORE *Shit*

CONTINUE VENTING AND/OR EXPLORE THE POSSIBILITY THAT THERE MIGHT ACTUALLY BE A SILVER-LINING IN ALL OF THIS.

_____
_____
_____
_____
_____
_____

What Can I do to unclusterfuck tomorrow?

_____
_____
_____
_____
_____
_____
_____
_____
_____
_____

GET SHIT DONE!

ACCOMPLISHING TASKS ARE A GREAT WAY TO FEEL BETTER. LIST THINGS THAT NEED TO GET DONE & DO IT!

1.
2.
3.
4.
5.

HAPPY THOUGHT OF THE DAY...

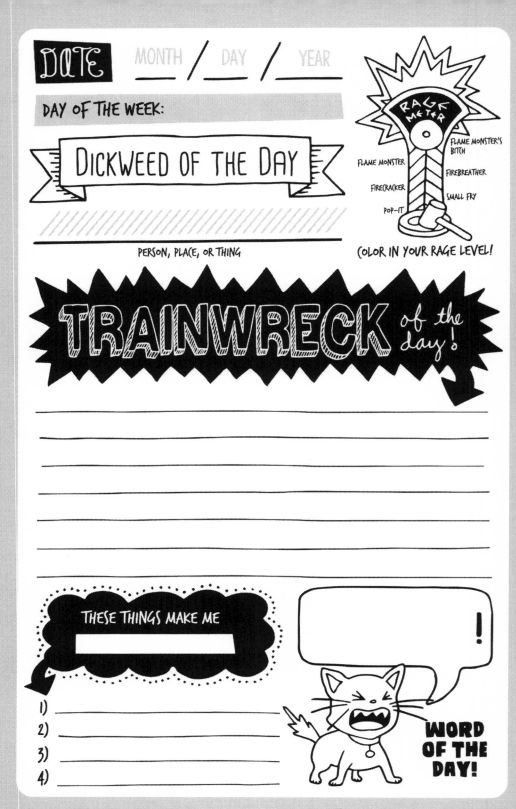

DATE ___ MONTH / ___ DAY / ___ YEAR

DAY OF THE WEEK:

DICKWEED OF THE DAY

PERSON, PLACE, OR THING

RAGE METER

FLAME MONSTER'S BITCH
FLAME MONSTER
FIREBREATHER
FIRECRACKER
SMALL FRY
POP-IT

COLOR IN YOUR RAGE LEVEL!

TRAINWRECK of the day!

THESE THINGS MAKE ME _____

1) _____
2) _____
3) _____
4) _____

!

WORD OF THE DAY!

MORE *Shit*

What Can I do to unclusterfuck tomorrow?

THESE WORDS MAKE ME HAPPY...

1.
2.
3.
4.
5.

HAPPY THOUGHT OF THE DAY...

DATE

DAY OF THE WEEK:

FUCKFACE OF THE DAY

PERSON, PLACE, OR THING

500
400
300
200
100

RAGE METER

COLOR IN YOUR RAGE LEVEL!

SHITSTORM of the day!

I DON'T GIVE A RAT'S ASS ABOUT...

!

1) _____
2) _____
3) _____
4) _____

WORD OF THE DAY!

MORE *Shit*

CONTINUE VENTING AND/OR EXPLORE THE POSSIBILITY THAT THERE MIGHT ACTUALLY BE A SILVER-LINING IN ALL OF THIS.

_____
_____
_____
_____
_____
_____

What Can I do to unclusterfuck tomorrow?

_____
_____
_____
_____
_____
_____
_____
_____
_____
_____
_____
_____

GET SHIT DONE!

ACCOMPLISHING TASKS ARE A GREAT WAY TO FEEL BETTER. LIST THINGS THAT NEED TO GET DONE & DO IT!

1.
2.
3.
4.
5.

HAPPY THOUGHT OF THE DAY...

DATE MONTH / DAY / YEAR

DAY OF THE WEEK:

Bitch of the Day

PERSON, PLACE, OR THING

NEED TO KILL SOMETHING!

BOILING OVER

ON EDGE

RAGE METER

COLOR IN YOUR RAGE LEVEL!

FLUSTERCLUCK of the day!

RELEASE FRUSTRATION. SCRIBBLE LIKE MAD!

!

WORD OF THE DAY!

MORE *Shit*

CONTINUE VENTING AND/OR EXPLORE THE POSSIBILITY THAT THERE MIGHT ACTUALLY BE A SILVER-LINING IN ALL OF THIS.

_____
_____
_____
_____
_____
_____

What Can I do to unclusterfuck tomorrow?

_____
_____
_____
_____
_____
_____
_____
_____
_____
_____
_____
_____
_____
_____

THESE _____ MAKE ME FEEL HAPPY.

1.
2.
3.
4.
5.

HAPPY THOUGHT OF THE DAY...

DATE MONTH / DAY / YEAR
___ / ___ / ___

DAY OF THE WEEK:

ASSHOLE OF THE DAY

PERSON, PLACE, OR THING

RAGE-O-METER

COLOR IN YOUR RAGE LEVEL!

CLUSTERFUCK of the day!

_____
_____
_____
_____
_____
_____

THESE THINGS MAKE ME WANT TO PUNCH MY PILLOW...

1) _____
2) _____
3) _____
4) _____

!

WORD OF THE DAY!

MORE *Shit*

What Can I do to unclusterfuck tomorrow?

I'M FUCKING LUCKY TO HAVE...
LIST PEOPLE AND/OR THINGS THAT YOU ARE GRATEFUL FOR.

1.
2.
3.
4.
5.

HAPPY THOUGHT OF THE DAY...

DATE ___ MONTH / ___ DAY / ___ YEAR

DAY OF THE WEEK:

Cumtart of the Day

//

PERSON, PLACE, OR THING

COLOR IN YOUR RAGE LEVEL!

RAGE METER

SHITFEST of the day!

_____
_____
_____
_____
_____
_____
_____

♫ ♫ CRAPPY DAY MUSIC PLAYLIST...

1) _____
2) _____
3) _____
4) _____

!

WORD OF THE DAY!

MORE *Shit*

CONTINUE VENTING AND/OR EXPLORE THE POSSIBILITY THAT THERE MIGHT ACTUALLY BE A SILVER-LINING IN ALL OF THIS.

_____
_____
_____
_____
_____
_____
_____
_____

What Can I do to unclusterfuck tomorrow?

_____
_____
_____
_____
_____
_____
_____
_____
_____
_____
_____
_____

GET SHIT DONE!

ACCOMPLISHING TASKS ARE A GREAT WAY TO FEEL BETTER. LIST THINGS THAT NEED TO GET DONE & DO IT!

1.
2.
3.
4.
5.

HAPPY THOUGHT OF THE DAY...

DATE

MONTH / DAY / YEAR

_____ / _____ / _____

DAY OF THE WEEK:

DICKWEED OF THE DAY

PERSON, PLACE, OR THING

RAGE METER

FLAME MONSTER'S BITCH

FLAME MONSTER

FIREBREATHER

FIRECRACKER

SMALL FRY

POP-IT

COLOR IN YOUR RAGE LEVEL!

TRAINWRECK of the day!

_____

_____

_____

_____

_____

_____

_____

THESE THINGS MAKE ME _____

1) _____

2) _____

3) _____

4) _____

!

WORD OF THE DAY!

MORE *Shit*

CONTINUE VENTING AND/OR EXPLORE THE POSSIBILITY THAT THERE MIGHT ACTUALLY BE A SILVER-LINING IN ALL OF THIS.

What Can I do to unclusterfuck tomorrow?

THESE WORDS MAKE ME HAPPY...

1.
2.
3.
4.
5.

HAPPY THOUGHT OF THE DAY...

DATE
MONTH / DAY / YEAR

DAY OF THE WEEK: ___

FUCKFACE OF THE DAY

PERSON, PLACE, OR THING

RAGE METER
SWAT   PUNCH   NUKE

DRAW IN THE NEEDLE!

SHITSTORM of the day!

_____
_____
_____
_____
_____
_____

I DON'T GIVE A RAT'S ASS ABOUT...

1) _____
2) _____
3) _____
4) _____

!

WORD OF THE DAY!

MORE *Shit*

CONTINUE VENTING AND/OR EXPLORE THE POSSIBILITY THAT THERE MIGHT ACTUALLY BE A SILVER-LINING IN ALL OF THIS.

_____
_____
_____
_____
_____
_____
_____

What Can I do to unclusterfuck tomorrow?

_____
_____
_____
_____
_____
_____
_____
_____
_____
_____
_____
_____
_____
_____

GET SHIT DONE!
ACCOMPLISHING TASKS ARE A GREAT WAY TO FEEL BETTER. LIST THINGS THAT NEED TO GET DONE & DO IT!

1.
2.
3.
4.
5.

HAPPY THOUGHT OF THE DAY...

DAY OF THE WEEK:

Bitch of the Day

//////////////////////////////////////

PERSON, PLACE, OR THING

RAGE METER

FIRE
HOT
MILD

COLOR IN YOUR RAGE LEVEL!

FLUSTERCLUCK of the day!

_____

_____

_____

_____

_____

_____

RELEASE FRUSTRATION. SCRIBBLE LIKE MAD!

!

WORD OF THE DAY!

MORE *Shit*

CONTINUE VENTING AND/OR EXPLORE THE POSSIBILITY THAT THERE MIGHT ACTUALLY BE A SILVER-LINING IN ALL OF THIS.

_____
_____
_____
_____
_____
_____
_____

What Can I do to unclusterfuck tomorrow?

_____
_____
_____
_____
_____
_____
_____
_____
_____
_____
_____

THESE [   ] MAKE ME FEEL HAPPY.

1.
2.
3.
4.
5.

HAPPY THOUGHT OF THE DAY...

DATE ___ MONTH / ___ DAY / ___ YEAR

DAY OF THE WEEK:

ASSHOLE OF THE DAY

PERSON, PLACE, OR THING

RAGE METER

COLOR IN YOUR RAGE LEVEL!

CLUSTERFUCK of the day!

_____
_____
_____
_____
_____
_____
_____

THESE THINGS MAKE ME WANT TO PUNCH MY PILLOW...

1) _____
2) _____
3) _____
4) _____

!

WORD OF THE DAY!

MORE *Shit*

CONTINUE VENTING AND/OR EXPLORE THE POSSIBILITY THAT THERE MIGHT ACTUALLY BE A SILVER-LINING IN ALL OF THIS.

What Can I do to unclusterfuck tomorrow?

I'M FUCKING LUCKY TO HAVE...
LIST PEOPLE AND/OR THINGS THAT YOU ARE GRATEFUL FOR.

1.
2.
3.
4.
5.

HAPPY THOUGHT OF THE DAY...

DATE

MONTH / DAY / YEAR
____ / ____ / ____

DAY OF THE WEEK:

Cumtart of the Day

//

PERSON, PLACE, OR THING

RAGE METER

COLOR IN YOUR RAGE LEVEL!

SHITFEST of the day!

_____
_____
_____
_____
_____
_____
_____

CRAPPY DAY MUSIC PLAYLIST...

1) _____
2) _____
3) _____
4) _____

!

WORD OF THE DAY!

MORE *Shit*

CONTINUE VENTING AND/OR EXPLORE THE POSSIBILITY THAT THERE MIGHT ACTUALLY BE A SILVER-LINING IN ALL OF THIS.

_____
_____
_____
_____
_____
_____

What Can I do to unclusterfuck tomorrow?

_____
_____
_____
_____
_____
_____
_____
_____
_____
_____
_____
_____
_____

GET SHIT DONE!

ACCOMPLISHING TASKS ARE A GREAT WAY TO FEEL BETTER. LIST THINGS THAT NEED TO GET DONE & DO IT!

1.
2.
3.
4.
5.

HAPPY THOUGHT OF THE DAY...

DATE

MONTH / DAY / YEAR

___ / ___ / ___

DAY OF THE WEEK:

DICKWEED OF THE DAY

//

PERSON, PLACE, OR THING

RAGE METER

FLAME MONSTER'S BITCH

FLAME MONSTER

FIREBREATHER

FIRECRACKER

SMALL FRY

POP-IT

COLOR IN YOUR RAGE LEVEL!

TRAINWRECK of the day!

_____
_____
_____
_____
_____
_____

THESE THINGS MAKE ME

_____

1) _____
2) _____
3) _____
4) _____

!

WORD OF THE DAY!

MORE *Shit*

CONTINUE VENTING AND/OR EXPLORE THE POSSIBILITY THAT THERE MIGHT ACTUALLY BE A SILVER-LINING IN ALL OF THIS.

_____

_____

_____

_____

_____

_____

_____

What Can I do to unclusterfuck tomorrow?

_____

_____

_____

_____

_____

_____

_____

_____

_____

_____

_____

_____

_____

THESE WORDS MAKE ME HAPPY...

1.

2.

3.

4.

5.

HAPPY THOUGHT OF THE DAY...

DATE

MONTH ___ / DAY ___ / YEAR ___

DAY OF THE WEEK: _____

FUCKFACE OF THE DAY

//

PERSON, PLACE, OR THING

RAGE METER

500
400
300
200
100

COLOR IN YOUR RAGE LEVEL!

SHITSTORM of the day!

_____
_____
_____
_____
_____
_____

I DON'T GIVE A RAT'S ASS ABOUT...

1) _____
2) _____
3) _____
4) _____

!

WORD OF THE DAY!

MORE *Shit*

CONTINUE VENTING AND/OR EXPLORE THE POSSIBILITY THAT THERE MIGHT ACTUALLY BE A SILVER-LINING IN ALL OF THIS.

What Can I do to unclusterfuck tomorrow?

GET SHIT DONE!

ACCOMPLISHING TASKS ARE A GREAT WAY TO FEEL BETTER. LIST THINGS THAT NEED TO GET DONE & DO IT!

1.
2.
3.
4.
5.

HAPPY THOUGHT OF THE DAY...

DATE ___ MONTH / ___ DAY / ___ YEAR

DAY OF THE WEEK:

Bitch of the Day

PERSON, PLACE, OR THING

NEED TO KILL SOMETHING!

BOILING OVER

ON EDGE

RAGE METER

COLOR IN YOUR RAGE LEVEL!

FLUSTERCLUCK of the day!

RELEASE FRUSTRATION. SCRIBBLE LIKE MAD!

!

WORD OF THE DAY!

MORE *Shit*

CONTINUE VENTING AND/OR EXPLORE THE POSSIBILITY THAT THERE MIGHT ACTUALLY BE A SILVER-LINING IN ALL OF THIS.

_____

_____

_____

_____

_____

_____

_____

What Can I do to unclusterfuck tomorrow?

_____

_____

_____

_____

_____

_____

_____

_____

_____

_____

_____

_____

_____

THESE _____ MAKE ME FEEL HAPPY.

1.

2.

3.

4.

5.

HAPPY THOUGHT OF THE DAY...

DAY OF THE WEEK:

ASSHOLE OF THE DAY

//

PERSON, PLACE, OR THING

RAGE-O-METER

COLOR IN YOUR RAGE LEVEL!

CLUSTERFUCK of the day!

_____

_____

_____

_____

_____

_____

THESE THINGS MAKE ME WANT TO PUNCH MY PILLOW...

1) _____

2) _____

3) _____

4) _____

!

WORD OF THE DAY!

MORE *Shit*

CONTINUE VENTING AND/OR EXPLORE THE POSSIBILITY THAT THERE MIGHT ACTUALLY BE A SILVER-LINING IN ALL OF THIS.

_____

_____

_____

_____

_____

_____

_____

What Can I do to unclusterfuck tomorrow?

_____

_____

_____

_____

_____

_____

_____

_____

_____

_____

_____

_____

I'M FUCKING LUCKY TO HAVE...

LIST PEOPLE AND/OR THINGS THAT YOU ARE GRATEFUL FOR.

1.

2.

3.

4.

5.

HAPPY THOUGHT OF THE DAY...

DAY OF THE WEEK:

Cumtart of the Day

PERSON, PLACE, OR THING

COLOR IN YOUR RAGE LEVEL!

RAGE METER

SHITFEST of the day!

_____
_____
_____
_____
_____
_____
_____

♫ CRAPPY DAY MUSIC PLAYLIST... ♫

1) _____
2) _____
3) _____
4) _____

!

WORD OF THE DAY!

MORE *Shit*

CONTINUE VENTING AND/OR EXPLORE THE POSSIBILITY THAT THERE MIGHT ACTUALLY BE A SILVER-LINING IN ALL OF THIS.

_____

_____

_____

_____

_____

_____

_____

What Can I do to unclusterfuck tomorrow?

_____

_____

_____

_____

_____

_____

_____

_____

_____

GET SHIT DONE!
ACCOMPLISHING TASKS ARE A GREAT WAY TO FEEL BETTER. LIST THINGS THAT NEED TO GET DONE & DO IT!

1.

2.

3.

4.

5.

HAPPY THOUGHT OF THE DAY...

DATE MONTH / DAY / YEAR
____ / ____ / ____

DAY OF THE WEEK:

DICKWEED OF THE DAY

//

PERSON, PLACE, OR THING

RAGE METER

FLAME MONSTER'S BITCH
FLAME MONSTER
FIREBREATHER
FIRECRACKER
SMALL FRY
POP-IT

COLOR IN YOUR RAGE LEVEL!

TRAINWRECK of the day!

_____

_____

_____

_____

_____

_____

THESE THINGS MAKE ME
_____

!

1) _____
2) _____
3) _____
4) _____

WORD OF THE DAY!

MORE *Shit*

CONTINUE VENTING AND/OR EXPLORE THE POSSIBILITY THAT THERE MIGHT ACTUALLY BE A SILVER-LINING IN ALL OF THIS.

_____

_____

_____

_____

_____

_____

_____

What can I do to unclusterfuck tomorrow?

_____

_____

_____

_____

_____

_____

_____

_____

_____

_____

_____

THESE WORDS MAKE ME HAPPY...

1.

2.

3.

4.

5.

HAPPY THOUGHT OF THE DAY...

DATE MONTH / DAY / YEAR ___ / ___ / ___

DAY OF THE WEEK: _____

FUCKFACE OF THE DAY

PERSON, PLACE, OR THING

RAGE METER

DRAW IN THE NEEDLE!

SHITSTORM of the day!

_____
_____
_____
_____
_____

I DON'T GIVE A RAT'S ASS ABOUT...

1) _____
2) _____
3) _____
4) _____

WORD OF THE DAY!

MORE *Shit*

CONTINUE VENTING AND/OR EXPLORE THE POSSIBILITY THAT THERE MIGHT ACTUALLY BE A SILVER-LINING IN ALL OF THIS.

What Can I do to unclusterfuck tomorrow?

GET SHIT DONE!
ACCOMPLISHING TASKS ARE A GREAT WAY TO FEEL BETTER. LIST THINGS THAT NEED TO GET DONE & DO IT!

1.
2.
3.
4.
5.

HAPPY THOUGHT OF THE DAY...

DATE MONTH / DAY / YEAR
_____ / _____ / _____

DAY OF THE WEEK:

Bitch of the Day

//////////////////////////////////

PERSON, PLACE, OR THING

RAGE METER

FIRE

HOT

MILD

COLOR IN YOUR RAGE LEVEL!

FLUSTERCLUCK of the day!

_____
_____
_____
_____
_____
_____

RELEASE FRUSTRATION.
SCRIBBLE LIKE MAD!

!

WORD OF THE DAY!

MORE *Shit*

CONTINUE VENTING AND/OR EXPLORE THE POSSIBILITY THAT THERE MIGHT ACTUALLY BE A SILVER-LINING IN ALL OF THIS.

_____

_____

_____

_____

_____

_____

_____

What Can I do to unclusterfuck tomorrow?

_____

_____

_____

_____

_____

_____

_____

_____

_____

_____

_____

_____

_____

THESE _____ MAKE ME FEEL HAPPY.

1.

2.

3.

4.

5.

HAPPY THOUGHT OF THE DAY...

DATE MONTH ___ / DAY ___ / YEAR ___

DAY OF THE WEEK: _____

ASSHOLE OF THE DAY

//

PERSON, PLACE, OR THING

RAGE-O-METER

COLOR IN YOUR RAGE LEVEL!

CLUSTERFUCK of the day!

_____

_____

_____

_____

_____

_____

THESE THINGS MAKE ME WANT TO PUNCH MY PILLOW...

1) _____

2) _____

3) _____

4) _____

!

WORD OF THE DAY!

MORE *Shit*

CONTINUE VENTING AND/OR EXPLORE THE POSSIBILITY THAT THERE MIGHT ACTUALLY BE A SILVER-LINING IN ALL OF THIS.

What Can I do to unclusterfuck tomorrow?

I'M FUCKING LUCKY TO HAVE...
LIST PEOPLE AND/OR THINGS THAT YOU ARE GRATEFUL FOR.

1.
2.
3.
4.
5.

HAPPY THOUGHT OF THE DAY...

DATE

MONTH / DAY / YEAR

___/___/___

DAY OF THE WEEK: _____

Cumtart of the Day

//

PERSON, PLACE, OR THING

COLOR IN YOUR RAGE LEVEL!

RAGE METER

SHITFEST of the day!

_____
_____
_____
_____
_____
_____

CRAPPY DAY MUSIC PLAYLIST...

1) _____
2) _____
3) _____
4) _____

!

WORD OF THE DAY!

MORE *Shit*

CONTINUE VENTING AND/OR EXPLORE THE POSSIBILITY THAT THERE MIGHT ACTUALLY BE A SILVER-LINING IN ALL OF THIS.

_____

_____

_____

_____

_____

_____

_____

What Can I do to unclusterfuck tomorrow?

_____

_____

_____

_____

_____

_____

_____

_____

_____

_____

_____

GET SHIT DONE!

ACCOMPLISHING TASKS ARE A GREAT WAY TO FEEL BETTER. LIST THINGS THAT NEED TO GET DONE & DO IT!

1.

2.

3.

4.

5.

HAPPY THOUGHT OF THE DAY...

DAY OF THE WEEK:

DICKWEED OF THE DAY

//////////////////////////////

PERSON, PLACE, OR THING

RAGE METER

FLAME MONSTER'S BITCH

FLAME MONSTER

FIREBREATHER

FIRECRACKER

SMALL FRY

POP-IT

COLOR IN YOUR RAGE LEVEL!

TRAINWRECK *of the day!*

_____
_____
_____
_____
_____

THESE THINGS MAKE ME

_____

1) _____
2) _____
3) _____
4) _____

!

WORD OF THE DAY!

MORE *Shit*

CONTINUE VENTING AND/OR EXPLORE THE POSSIBILITY THAT THERE MIGHT ACTUALLY BE A SILVER-LINING IN ALL OF THIS.

_____
_____
_____
_____
_____
_____
_____

What Can I do to unclusterfuck tomorrow?

THESE WORDS MAKE ME HAPPY...

_____
_____
_____

1.
2.
3.
4.
5.

_____
_____
_____
_____
_____
_____
_____
_____
_____
_____
_____

HAPPY THOUGHT OF THE DAY...

DATE MONTH / DAY / YEAR ___ / ___ / ___

DAY OF THE WEEK:

FUCKFACE OF THE DAY

PERSON, PLACE, OR THING

RAGE METER

500
400
300
200
100

COLOR IN YOUR RAGE LEVEL!

SHITSTORM of the day!

I DON'T GIVE A RAT'S ASS ABOUT...

1) _____
2) _____
3) _____
4) _____

!

WORD OF THE DAY!

MORE *Shit*

CONTINUE VENTING AND/OR EXPLORE THE POSSIBILITY THAT THERE MIGHT ACTUALLY BE A SILVER-LINING IN ALL OF THIS.

_____
_____
_____
_____
_____
_____
_____

What Can I do to unclusterfuck tomorrow?

_____
_____
_____
_____
_____
_____
_____
_____
_____
_____
_____

GET SHIT DONE!
ACCOMPLISHING TASKS ARE A GREAT WAY TO FEEL BETTER. LIST THINGS THAT NEED TO GET DONE & DO IT!

1.
2.
3.
4.
5.

HAPPY THOUGHT OF THE DAY...

CHECK OUT MY SWEAR WORD ADULT COLORING BOOKS
AT: SWEARWORDCOLORINGBOOK.COM!

Made in the USA
Coppell, TX
04 May 2023

16428481R00062